Clementine A. Fortier

interesting facts to make you look crazy smart

Contents

  1.

  2.

  3.

  4.

  5.

  6.

  7.

  8.

  9.

  10.

1

Introduction

Embark on a thrilling journey into the realm of intellectual curiosity with "Interesting Facts to Make You Look Crazy Smart." Brace yourself for a mind-bending exploration of the extraordinary, the unexpected, and the utterly fascinating. In this captivating compendium, we unravel the secrets that will not only amaze but elevate your intellectual prowess to unprecedented heights.

Prepare to be astounded as we delve into a tapestry of mind-blowing facts, meticulously curated to ignite your curiosity and leave you utterly mesmerized. From the marvels of science to the quirks of history, each page is a portal to a world where the ordinary transforms into the extraordinary. These facts are not just tidbits of information; they are the keys to unlocking the doors of perception, revealing the hidden wonders that surround us.

Ever wondered about the perplexing mysteries of the universe? Brace yourself for revelations that will leave you questioning everything you thought you knew. Discover the captivating stories behind historical events that shaped the course of humanity, and let the narratives of the past unveil the secrets they've long held.

But this book is more than a mere collection of facts—it's a tool for transforming ordinary conversations into extraordinary exchanges. Picture the scene: you effortlessly dropping astonishing knowledge bombs, leaving your audience in awe. Each fact is not just a nugget of information; it's a conversation starter, a glimpse into the extraordinary, and a chance to make an indelible impression.

"Interesting Facts to Make You Look Crazy Smart" is your passport to becoming the most intriguing person in the room. Let the journey begin, and get ready to amaze yourself and those around you with the dazzling gems of knowledge that await within these pages. Get ready to be the genius everyone admires!

2

Inventors and invention

1. The word "invention" comes from the Latin word "inventio," meaning a finding or discovery.
2. Archimedes, the ancient Greek mathematician, is credited with inventing the water screw, a device for raising water.
3. Leonardo da Vinci conceptualized inventions such as the helicopter and the tank centuries before they became a reality.
4. Thomas Edison held over 1,000 patents, including the phonograph, motion pictures, and the incandescent light bulb.
5. The first recorded patent in history was granted in 1421 to Filippo Brunelleschi for a barge with hoisting gear.
6. The invention of the printing press by Johannes Gutenberg in 1440 revolutionized the spread of knowledge and information.
7. The safety razor, a common bathroom item, was invented by King C. Gillette in 1901.
8. The invention of the internet is attributed to Sir Tim Berners-Lee, who proposed the World Wide Web in 1989.
9. The concept of the electric car dates back to the 19th century, with inventors like Thomas Parker creating early prototypes.
10. The first practical typewriter was patented in 1868 by Christopher Latham Sholes, Samuel Soule, and Carlos Glidden.
11. The Wright brothers, Orville and Wilbur, are credited with inventing and building the world's first successful airplane in 1903.
12. Marie Curie, the Nobel Prize-winning scientist, invented the portable X-ray machine during World War I.
13. The microwave oven was invented accidentally by Percy Spencer in 1945 while working on radar technology.
14. Velcro was inspired by burrs sticking to clothing, leading Swiss engineer George de Mestral to invent it in 1948.
15. The concept of 3D printing was first introduced by Chuck Hull in 1986, revolutionizing manufacturing processes.

16. The first practical telephone was patented by Alexander Graham Bell in 1876.

17. The concept of the credit card was invented by Ralph Schneider and Frank McNamara in 1950.

18. George Washington Carver, an African American botanist, invented over 300 products using peanuts, including peanut butter.

19. The first computer mouse was invented by Douglas Engelbart in 1963, revolutionizing computer interactions.

20. The disposable diaper was invented by Marion Donovan in 1950.

21. The concept of the barcode was invented by Norman Joseph Woodland and Bernard Silver in 1952.

22. The Post-it note was invented by Spencer Silver and Arthur Fry in 1974 at 3M.

23. The Frisbee was invented by Walter Morrison in 1948 as a pie tin, later becoming a popular recreational toy.

24. The first modern bicycle, known as the "safety bicycle," was invented by John Kemp Starley in 1885.

25. The world's first electric washing machine was invented by Alva J. Fisher in 1908.

26. The invention of Velcro was inspired by burrs sticking to clothing.

27. The concept of GPS was developed by the United States Department of Defense and became fully operational in 1995.

28. The first successful human heart transplant was performed by Dr. Christiaan Barnard in 1967.

29. The concept of the pacemaker was developed by Wilson Greatbatch in 1958.

30. The invention of the pacemaker was inspired by a mistake made by Wilson Greatbatch in the lab.

31. The concept of the artificial heart was developed by Dr. Robert Jarvik in 1982.

32. The first successful in vitro fertilization (IVF) was performed by Dr. Robert Edwards and Dr. Patrick Steptoe in 1978.

33. The concept of the laser was developed by Theodore Maiman in 1960.

34. The concept of the first digital camera was developed by Steven Sasson at Kodak in 1975.

35. The concept of the computer mouse was developed by Douglas Engelbart in 1963.

36. The concept of the World Wide Web was proposed by Sir Tim Berners-Lee in 1989.

37. The first practical electric car was built by Thomas Parker in 1889.

38. The concept of the MRI machine was developed by Raymond Damadian in 1977.

39. The first successful kidney transplant was performed by Dr. Joseph E. Murray in 1954.

40. The concept of the electric guitar was developed by George Beauchamp in 1931.

41. The first successful penicillin treatment was administered by Sir Alexander Fleming in 1928.

42. The concept of the defibrillator was developed by Dr. Paul Zoll in the 1950s.

43. The first successful organ transplant (kidney) was performed by Dr. Joseph E. Murray in 1954.

44. The concept of the first practical video game was developed by William Higinbotham in 1958.

45. The concept of the LED was developed by Nick Holonyak Jr. in 1962.

46. The concept of the first practical television was developed by Philo Farnsworth in 1927.

47. The concept of the first practical telephone was developed by Alexander Graham Bell in 1876.

48. The first successful open-heart surgery was performed by Dr. C. Walton Lillehei in 1952.

49. The concept of the first practical car was developed by Karl Benz in 1885.

50. The concept of the first practical airplane was developed by the Wright brothers in 1903.

51. The concept of the first practical sewing machine was developed by Elias Howe in 1846.

52. The first successful artificial heart transplant was performed by Dr. Denton Cooley in 1969.

53. The concept of the first practical refrigerator was developed by Jacob Perkins in 1834.

54. The concept of the first practical light bulb was developed by Thomas Edison in 1879.

55. The first successful test-tube baby was born through in vitro fertilization (IVF) in 1978.

56. The concept of the first practical steam engine was developed by Thomas Savery in 1698.

57. The concept of the first practical steam locomotive was developed by George Stephenson in 1814.

58. The first successful liver transplant was performed by Dr. Thomas Starzl in 1967.

59. The concept of the first practical submarine was developed by Cornelius Drebbel in 1620.

60. The concept of the first practical bicycle was developed by Karl Drais in 1817.

61. The first successful cochlear implant surgery was performed by Dr. William House in 1961.

62. The concept of the first practical escalator was developed by Jesse Reno in 1891.

63. The concept of the first practical fax machine was developed by Alexander Bain in 1843.

64. The first successful heart-lung transplant was performed by Dr. Bruce Reitz in 1981.

65. The concept of the first practical helicopter was developed by Igor Sikorsky in 1939.

66. The first successful cornea transplant was performed by Sir Archibald McIndoe in 1944.

67. The concept of the first practical jet engine was developed by Sir Frank Whittle in 1930.

3

Airplanes and airports

1. The Boeing 747 has about six million parts, including bolts and rivets.
2. The Wright brothers' first powered flight in 1903 covered a distance shorter than the wingspan of a Boeing 747.
3. The Airbus A380 is the world's largest passenger aircraft, capable of carrying over 800 passengers.
4. The fastest speed recorded by a commercial airliner is around 1,354 miles per hour by the Concorde.
5. The Boeing 777 is often called the "Triple Seven" because of its 7,000-kilometer range, 7 feet in diameter engines, and 7-foot wingspan extensions.
6. The Boeing 787 Dreamliner is made of 50% composite materials, making it lighter and more fuel-efficient.
7. The world's busiest airport is Hartsfield-Jackson Atlanta International Airport.
8. The shortest commercial flight in the world is between Westray and Papa Westray in Scotland, lasting only 47 seconds.
9. The Airbus A350 XWB features larger windows to reduce jet lag by allowing more natural light.
10. The Antonov An-225 Mriya is the world's largest cargo plane, with a wingspan of 88.4 meters.
11. Hong Kong International Airport has a golf course, making it the only airport with this unique facility.
12. The Concorde could fly at Mach 2, more than twice the speed of sound.
13. The longest non-stop commercial flight is from Singapore to Newark, covering a distance of approximately 9,534 miles.
14. Some airplane tires are filled with nitrogen instead of regular air to prevent combustion during a fire.
15. The Airbus A340 has more than 500 miles of wiring inside it.
16. The world's largest passenger terminal is in Dubai at the Al Maktoum International Airport.
17. The Boeing 747's engines are wide enough for a Boeing 737 to fly through.
18. The first flight attendants were registered nurses.

19. There is a hidden city in the U.S. where flights are cheaper due to airline routing.

20. The fastest military jet, the SR-71 Blackbird, can fly at speeds exceeding Mach 3.

21. The term "black box" is misleading; flight recorders are usually orange to make them easier to find.

22. Singapore Airlines offers the most extended non-stop flight, which lasts about 18 hours from Singapore to Newark.

23. The busiest air route is between Seoul and Jeju Island in South Korea.

24. The world's highest commercial airport is Daocheng Yading Airport in China, situated at 14,472 feet above sea level.

25. The first woman to fly solo around the world was Geraldine Mock in 1964.

26. The Boeing 737 is the best-selling commercial jet of all time.

27. The longest-running non-stop flight by distance is from Sydney to Dallas, covering approximately 8,577 miles.

28. The word "Mayday" used in distress calls comes from the French word "m'aider," which means "help me."

29. The International Air Transport Association (IATA) code for airports comes from the initial letter(s) of the city or airport name.

30. The first-class section on a plane is a result of the Hindenburg airship's luxurious accommodations.

31. The world's highest air traffic control tower is in Tibet, at an elevation of 14,219 feet.

32. The Boeing 747's distinctive hump was originally designed to carry cargo.

33. The Boeing 747 can carry about 57,285 gallons of fuel.

34. The longest domestic flight in the U.S. is from Boston to Honolulu, covering approximately 5,099 miles.

35. The first controlled, sustained, powered flight by the Wright brothers lasted only 12 seconds.

36. The shortest international flight is between Gibraltar and Tangier, lasting around 20 minutes.

37. The term "jet lag" was first coined in 1966.

38. The busiest day ever for air travel was on July 24, 2019, with over 230,000 flights recorded worldwide.

39. The world's highest-altitude airport is Daocheng Yading Airport in China.

40. The first woman to earn a pilot's license was Raymonde de Laroche in 1910.

41. The highest number of takeoffs and landings in 24 hours by a single aircraft is 100, as achieved by the Rutan Model 76 Voyager.

42. The longest continuously operating airline is KLM, founded in 1919.

43. The term "red-eye flight" refers to overnight flights due to passengers' tired, bloodshot eyes.

44. The Airbus A380's wingspan is longer than the aircraft itself.

45. The world's narrowest runway is located in the Courchevel Altiport in the French Alps.

46. The first flight attendant uniforms were designed to resemble nurses' uniforms to inspire confidence in passengers.

47. The world's largest air force is the United States Air Force.

48. The first flight around the world was completed in 1924 by a team of aviators in four Douglas World Cruisers.

49. The Boeing 787 Dreamliner can take off at a 5.5-degree angle.

50. The world's largest airshow is EAA AirVenture Oshkosh in Wisconsin, USA.

51. The term "jet engine" comes from the French word "réacteur," coined by aircraft designer René Lorin.

52. The longest runway in the world is at Qamdo Bamda Airport in China, measuring 5.5 miles.

53. The Airbus A380's wingspan is longer than the aircraft itself.

54. The world's smallest airport is in the Caribbean on the island of Saba.

55. The first commercial airline flight took place in 1914, between St. Petersburg and Tampa, Florida.

56. The first airport hotel opened at London's Croydon Airport in 1929.

57. The world's first air traffic control tower was built in Cleveland in 1930.

58. The shortest scheduled flight in the world is between Westray and Papa Westray in Scotland, lasting only two minutes.

59. The world's busiest cargo airport is Hong Kong International Airport.

60. The Antonov An-225 Mriya, the world's largest cargo plane, was originally built to transport the Soviet space shuttle.

61. The first in-flight movie was shown in 1921 on an Aeromarine Airways flight.

62. The largest airline by the number of destinations served is Turkish Airlines.

63. The world's fastest passenger aircraft, the Concorde, could fly at Mach 2.

64. The first woman to fly solo non-stop across the Atlantic was Amelia Earhart in 1932.

65. The Airbus A380 can carry approximately 81,890 gallons of fuel.

66. The first airport with a control tower was Cleveland Municipal Airport (now Cleveland Hopkins International Airport).

67. The first aircraft with a pressurized cabin was the Boeing 307 Stratoliner in 1938.

68. The longest non-stop passenger flight by duration is around 20 hours from New York to Sydney.

69. The Boeing 787 Dreamliner is the first commercial airplane to be made mostly of carbon composites.

70. The term "airplane mode" on smartphones was inspired by the need to turn off electronic devices during flights.

4

History and culture

1. The Great Wall of China is not visible from the Moon with the naked eye, contrary to popular belief.
2. Cleopatra, the last pharaoh of ancient Egypt, lived closer in time to the moon landing than to the construction of the Great Pyramid.
3. The oldest known map of the world is from ancient Babylon and dates back to the 6th century BCE.
4. The word "nerd" was first coined by Dr. Seuss in "If I Ran the Zoo" in 1950.
5. The ancient city of Rome had a 250-mile-long road system, the Appian Way, connecting it to other parts of Italy.
6. The first recorded Olympic Games were held in 776 BCE in Olympia, Greece.
7. The Eiffel Tower can be 15 cm taller during the summer due to the expansion of the iron in the heat.
8. The ancient city of Troy, featured in Homer's epic poems, was discovered by archaeologist Heinrich Schliemann in the 19th century.
9. The oldest known written language is Sumerian cuneiform, dating back to around 3200 BCE.
10. The Hanging Gardens of Babylon, one of the Seven Wonders of the Ancient World, might have never existed, according to some historians.
11. The Incas used a complex system of knotted strings called quipu for record-keeping and communication.
12. The shortest war in history was between Britain and Zanzibar in 1896, lasting only 38 minutes.
13. The Library of Alexandria, one of the largest and most significant libraries of the ancient world, was destroyed in multiple incidents, and its exact location remains uncertain.
14. The ancient city of Mohenjo-Daro in the Indus Valley had a sophisticated sewage and drainage system over 4,000 years ago.
15. The word "hello" was first used to greet someone by Thomas Edison to answer the phone.

16. The Great Sphinx of Giza has a nose missing, and the legend that Napoleon shot it off with a cannon is likely a myth.

17. The world's oldest known musical instruments, flutes made from bird bones and mammoth ivory, were discovered in a cave in Germany.

18. The concept of zero in mathematics originated in ancient India.

19. The phrase "crossing the Rubicon" refers to Julius Caesar's daring move to march his army across the Rubicon River in defiance of Roman law.

20. The ancient Greek philosopher Socrates never wrote down any of his teachings; they were recorded by his students, primarily Plato.

21. The Great Fire of London in 1666 was inadvertently started by a small flame in a bakery on Pudding Lane.

22. The Aztecs used cocoa beans as currency, and chocolate was reserved for the elite.

23. The Terracotta Army in China, created to accompany the first emperor in the afterlife, consists of over 8,000 life-sized soldiers and horses.

24. The shortest war in history was between Britain and Zanzibar in 1896, lasting only 38 minutes.

25. The iconic "V-J Day in Times Square" photograph, depicting a sailor kissing a nurse, was taken on August 14, 1945, marking the end of World War II.

26. The Great Emu War occurred in Australia in 1932 when the government declared war on emus due to their overpopulation damaging crops.

27. The ancient Greek city of Athens is named after the goddess Athena, who won a contest against Poseidon for the city's patronage.

28. The word "barbarian" originated from ancient Greeks who used it to describe non-Greek-speaking people whose language sounded like "bar-bar" to them.

29. The first known reference to soap dates back to ancient Babylon, where a recipe was inscribed on a clay tablet around 2200 BCE.

30. The tradition of wedding rings dates back to ancient Egypt, where they believed the ring finger had a vein that directly connected to the heart.

31. The Great Pyramid of Giza was originally covered in smooth, white Tura limestone casing stones, reflecting the sun's light and making it shine like a "gem" on the horizon.

32. The word "assassin" comes from the Arabic word "hashshashin," referring to a group of Nizari Ismailis who were known for their targeted killings.

33. The Inca Empire used a complex system of runners, known as chasquis, to transmit messages across vast distances.

34. The concept of democracy originated in ancient Greece, specifically in Athens, where citizens could participate in decision-making.

35. The tradition of shaking hands originated in ancient Greece as a gesture of showing that neither person was carrying a weapon.

36. The longest reigning monarch in history was King Sobhuza II of Swaziland, who ruled for 82 years from 1899 to 1982.

37. The first recorded joke dates back to ancient Sumeria around 1900 BCE.

38. The ancient Egyptians used honey as a natural antibiotic and to preserve mummies.

39. The word "salary" comes from the Latin word "salarium," which was a payment made to Roman soldiers to purchase salt.

40. The first known recipe is a Sumerian beer recipe from around 3900 BCE.

41. The Colosseum in Rome could be flooded to stage naval battles, known as naumachiae, for public entertainment.

42. The first public library was established in Athens in the 6th century BCE by the statesman Peisistratos.

43. The tradition of carving pumpkins for Halloween originated from the Irish, who used to carve turnips.

44. The oldest known board game is Senet, played in ancient Egypt over 5,000 years ago.

45. The word "trivia" comes from the Latin "trivium," which referred to the three foundational arts of grammar, rhetoric, and logic.

46. The ancient city of Pompeii was buried under ash and pumice after the eruption of Mount Vesuvius in 79 CE, preserving it remarkably well.

47. The concept of a seven-day week comes from ancient Babylon, where each day was associated with a celestial body.

48. The earliest known use of the word "computer" was in 1613, referring to a person who performed calculations.

49. The Hanging Gardens of Babylon may have been a mistranslation, and some historians believe they were located in Nineveh instead.

50. The ancient Greek city of Sparta had a unique system of government known as a diarchy, with two kings ruling simultaneously.

51. The Great Fire of London in 1666 was exacerbated by the city's narrow streets and buildings made of timber and thatch.

52. The famous painting "Starry Night" by Vincent van Gogh was created while he was in a mental institution.

53. The first recorded instance of graffiti dates back to ancient Egypt, where someone wrote a message on a wall in praise of a prostitute.

54. The oldest known written recipe is for beer and dates back to ancient Sumeria.

55. The ancient city of Carthage, a major power in the Mediterranean, was destroyed by the Romans in the Third Punic War.

56. The concept of the compass was invented by the Chinese during the Han Dynasty around the 2nd century BCE.

57. The Trojan Horse, as described in the Iliad, is believed by some historians to have been a battering ram rather than a wooden horse.

58. The ancient city of Petra in Jordan was rediscovered by a Swiss explorer in 1812 and is famous for its rock-cut architecture.

59. The tradition of April Fools' Day has uncertain origins but may be linked to the change of the calendar in the 16th century.

60. The ancient Mayans used a system of mathematics that included the concept of zero and advanced astronomical calculations.

61. The first recorded instance of dentistry comes from ancient Sumeria, where a text describes the treatment of toothaches.

62. The concept of the internet was proposed by J.C.R. Licklider in the early 1960s, envisioning a "galactic network" of computers.

63. The Great Zimbabwe, an ancient city in southeastern Africa, was the center of a powerful kingdom and a major trading hub.

64. The phrase "Let them eat cake" is often misattributed to Marie Antoinette and was likely never said by her.

65. The oldest known musical instrument is a bone flute dating back to the Upper Paleolithic period, over 35,000 years ago.

66. The ancient city of Byzantium was later renamed Constantinople and is now known as Istanbul.

67. The tradition of New Year's resolutions dates back to ancient Babylon, where people made promises to the gods at the start of the year.

68. The city of Venice was built on a network of wooden piles driven into the marshy ground.

69. The first recorded instance of a woman voting in the United States was Lydia Taft in 1756 in Massachusetts.

70. The concept of "guerrilla warfare" originated during the Peninsular War in the early 19th century, where small groups of fighters engaged in unconventional tactics against a larger force.

5

Animals

1. The tongue of a blue whale can weigh as much as an elephant.
2. Cows have best friends and can become stressed when they are separated.
3. A group of flamingos is called a "flamboyance."
4. The fingerprints of a koala are so indistinguishable from humans that they have been confused at crime scenes.
5. Honey never spoils. Archaeologists have found pots of honey in ancient Egyptian tombs that are over 3,000 years old and still perfectly edible.
6. Male seahorses are the ones that give birth and carry the eggs.
7. The lifespan of a dragonfly is just 24 hours.
8. A newborn kangaroo is the size of a lima bean.
9. A single elephant tooth can weigh as much as 9 pounds.
10. Penguins can jump up to 6 feet in the air.
11. The mimic octopus can imitate the appearance and behaviors of over 15 different marine species.
12. The heart of a shrimp is located in its head.
13. The cheetah is the fastest land animal, capable of reaching speeds up to 75 mph in short bursts.
14. A crocodile cannot stick its tongue out.
15. The tongue of a chameleon is twice the length of its body.
16. A group of owls is called a "parliament."
17. A newborn kangaroo stays in its mother's pouch for about 190 days.
18. An octopus has three hearts.
19. A snail can sleep for three years.
20. The fingerprints of a koala are so indistinguishable from humans that they have been confused at crime scenes.
21. The electric eel can generate shocks of up to 600 volts.
22. A newborn oyster is a male, and it can change its gender to female as it grows older.
23. The archerfish can spit water up to 5 feet to catch insects above the water's surface.

24. A giraffe's neck contains the same number of vertebrae as a human's.

25. The blue-ringed octopus carries enough venom to kill 26 adult humans within minutes.

26. Sloths take two weeks to digest their food.

27. The hydra, a tiny freshwater animal, is biologically immortal and can regenerate indefinitely.

28. The tongue of a giraffe is so long that it can clean its ears with it.

29. The narwhal's tusk is actually a long, spiral tooth that can grow up to 10 feet long.

30. Only female mosquitoes bite, as they need the protein from blood to lay their eggs.

31. The mimic octopus can imitate the appearance and behaviors of over 15 different marine species.

32. The only mammal capable of flight is the bat.

33. Elephants are the only animals that can't jump.

34. The hummingbird is the only bird that can fly backward.

35. The flying squirrel doesn't actually fly but glides using the skin between its front and hind legs.

36. A single strand of spider silk is thinner than a human hair but stronger than steel.

37. The tongue of a woodpecker wraps around its brain to protect it from the force of its hammering beak.

38. The laughing kookaburra's distinctive call sounds like laughter.

39. A group of ferrets is called a "business."

40. The star-nosed mole can eat and identify its food in less than a quarter of a second.

41. An adult human is made up of approximately 7,000,000,000,000,000,000,000,000,000 (7 octillion) atoms.

42. A shrimp's heart is in its head.

43. The quokka, a small Australian marsupial, is known as the world's happiest animal due to its smiling appearance.

44. The tongue of a blue whale can weigh as much as an elephant.

45. A newborn kangaroo stays in its mother's pouch for about 190 days.

46. The praying mantis is the only insect that can turn its head.

47. The sperm whale has the largest brain of any animal on Earth.

48. The axolotl, a salamander species, can regenerate its heart, brain, and other organs throughout its life.

49. The horn of a rhinoceros is made of keratin, the same substance as human hair and nails.

50. The bumblebee bat is the world's smallest mammal, weighing less than a penny.

51. A shrimp's heart is in its head.

52. The average housefly lives for about a month.

53. The aye-aye, a lemur species, has an elongated finger to extract insects from tree bark.

54. The thorny devil, a lizard native to Australia, can collect water by channeling it through grooves on its skin to its mouth.

55. A group of hedgehogs is called an "array."

56. The star-nosed mole can eat and identify its food in less than a quarter of a second.

57. A newborn kangaroo is the size of a lima bean.

58. The giraffe's long neck has the same number of vertebrae as a human's neck.

59. The Gila monster, a venomous lizard, is one of the few lizards that are capable of producing venom.

60. The pistol shrimp's snap can reach speeds of over 60 miles per hour and create a sound reaching 218 decibels, louder than a gunshot.

61. The slowest mammal is the three-toed sloth, which moves at a speed of about 0.03 miles per hour.

62. The axolotl, a salamander species, can regenerate its limbs, heart, and spinal cord.

63. The star-nosed mole can eat and identify its food in less than a quarter of a second.

64. The tongue of a giraffe is so long that it can clean its ears with it.

65. A group of crows is called a "murder."

66. The hummingbird is the only bird that can fly backward.

67. The basilisk lizard can run on water to escape predators, earning it the nickname "Jesus Christ lizard."

68. A group of jellyfish is called a "smack."

69. The kangaroo is the only large animal that uses hopping as its primary method of locomotion.

70. The only mammals capable of flight are bats.

6

Countries and cities

1. The Great Wall of China is visible from space, but only under certain conditions.
2. There are more than 3 million lakes in Canada, making it the country with the most lakes in the world.
3. Istanbul, Turkey, is the only city in the world that straddles two continents: Europe and Asia.
4. The world's highest motorable road is in India, reaching an elevation of 19,300 feet.
5. Russia spans 11 time zones, making it the country with the most time zones in the world.
6. Vatican City is the smallest country in the world, both in terms of size and population.
7. The Maldives is the lowest country on Earth, with an average ground level of just 4 feet 11 inches (1.5 meters) above sea level.
8. Monaco is the most densely populated country globally, with over 25,000 people per square kilometer.
9. The city of Rome has a sovereign nation, Vatican City, within its borders.
10. The world's largest desert is not the Sahara; it's Antarctica.
11. Bhutan is the only country in the world that measures its success by Gross National Happiness instead of Gross Domestic Product (GDP).
12. The Dead Sea, located between Jordan and Israel, is so salty that people can effortlessly float on its surface.
13. Australia is both a country and a continent.
14. Greenland is the largest island in the world, despite often being associated with continents.
15. There's a town named "Batman" in Turkey.
16. The city of Tokyo is the most populous metropolitan area globally, with over 37 million residents.
17. Norway has a population of around 5.3 million, and its residents speak more than 100 different languages.

18. Mount Everest, the world's highest peak, is still growing at a rate of about 4 millimeters per year.

19. More than 800 languages are spoken in Papua New Guinea, making it the most linguistically diverse country in the world.

20. The Great Barrier Reef in Australia is the largest coral reef system on the planet.

21. The city of Venice, Italy, is built on a network of canals, and its buildings are supported by wooden stakes.

22. Singapore is one of the cleanest cities globally and has strict laws against littering and gum chewing.

23. The Eiffel Tower can be 15 cm taller during the summer due to thermal expansion.

24. The city of Dubai in the United Arab Emirates has an indoor ski resort, Ski Dubai, despite its desert climate.

25. The Amazon Rainforest produces 20% of the world's oxygen.

26. Canada has the longest coastline of any country, stretching over 202,080 kilometers.

27. The city of Jerusalem is considered a holy city by three major world religions: Judaism, Christianity, and Islam.

28. The ancient city of Petra in Jordan is known for its rock-cut architecture and was featured in the film "Indiana Jones and the Last Crusade."

29. New York City's Central Park is larger than the principality of Monaco.

30. The city of Berlin, Germany, has more bridges than Venice, Italy.

31. The world's oldest continuously inhabited city is Damascus, Syria.

32. Finland has over 3 million saunas, roughly one for every two and a half people.

33. The world's largest flower, the Rafflesia Arnoldii, can be found in Indonesia and can grow up to three feet in diameter.

34. The city of Cape Town, South Africa, is home to the iconic Table Mountain, one of the New7Wonders of Nature.

35. Canada has more lakes than the rest of the world combined.

36. The city of Budapest, Hungary, is home to the third-largest parliament building globally.

37. Brazil is named after a tree, the Brazilwood, which was once the country's primary export.

38. The smallest country in Africa is Seychelles, an archipelago nation in the Indian Ocean.

39. Mount Kilimanjaro in Tanzania is the tallest free-standing mountain in the world.

40. The city of Seoul, South Korea, has a vibrant street food culture with dishes like tteokbokki and kimchi pancakes.

41. The United States has the most airports in the world.

42. In Iceland, there is a dating app that tells users if they are related to each other.

43. The city of Athens, Greece, is one of the oldest cities in the world, with a history spanning over 3,400 years.

44. Australia is home to the world's longest fence, the Dingo Fence, which stretches over 5,600 kilometers.

45. The city of Marrakech in Morocco is known for its vibrant marketplaces, called souks.

46. The island nation of Japan has 6,852 islands.

47. The city of Buenos Aires, Argentina, has the highest number of psychoanalysts per capita in the world.

48. The longest place name in the world is in New Zealand: Taumatawhakatangihangakoauauotamateaturipukakapikimaungahoronukupokaiw henuakitanatahu.

49. The city of Shanghai, China, has the world's fastest commercial train, reaching speeds of 431 km/h (268 mph).

50. Switzerland is known for its efficient public transportation system, including the famous Glacier Express.

51. The city of San Francisco, USA, is home to the Golden Gate Bridge, which was the world's longest suspension bridge when it opened in 1937.

52. Mount Vesuvius, near Naples, Italy, is the only active volcano on the European mainland.

53. Sweden has a "Freedom to Roam" policy, allowing people to camp and hike on any land, including private property.

54. The city of Nairobi, Kenya, is the only capital city in the world with a national park.

55. The city of Bangkok, Thailand, has the longest place name in the world in Thai.

56. The world's largest sand island, Fraser Island, is located off the coast of Australia.

57. The city of Prague, Czech Republic, has the largest ancient castle in the world.

58. Lake Baikal in Russia is the deepest freshwater lake globally, reaching depths of over 5,387 feet.

59. The city of Rio de Janeiro, Brazil, is home to the iconic Christ the Redeemer statue.

60. The city of Amsterdam, Netherlands, has more canals than Venice, Italy.

61. The city of Montreal, Canada, is the world's second-largest French-speaking city after Paris.

62. Mount Fuji in Japan is an active stratovolcano and is also the country's highest peak.

63. The city of Barcelona, Spain, has nine UNESCO World Heritage sites.

64. The city of Cairo, Egypt, is home to the world's oldest university, Al-Qarawiyyin University, founded in 859 AD.

65. The Great Pyramid of Giza in Egypt is the only one of the Seven Wonders of the Ancient World still in existence.

66. The city of Sydney, Australia, is surrounded by national parks, including the famous Blue Mountains.

67. The city of Beijing, China, is one of the most populous cities globally and has been the capital for over 800 years.

68. The island nation of Palau has one of the world's first shark sanctuaries.

69. The city of Vienna, Austria, is known for its classical music heritage and was home to composers like Mozart and Beethoven.

70. The city of Edinburgh, Scotland, has more than 4,500 historic buildings and monuments.

7

Language

1. There are approximately 7,000 languages spoken around the world.
2. The most widely spoken language is Mandarin Chinese, followed by English.
3. The word "alphabet" comes from the first two letters of the Greek alphabet: alpha and beta.
4. The longest word in the English language without a vowel is "rhythms."
5. The word "nerd" was first coined by Dr. Seuss in "If I Ran the Zoo" in 1950.
6. The word "bookkeeper" (and its variants) is the only unhyphenated English word with three consecutive double letters.
7. The word "hello" was originally used to convey surprise rather than greeting.
8. The Basque language, spoken in the Basque region of Spain and France, is unrelated to any other known language.
9. The sentence "The quick brown fox jumps over a lazy dog" uses every letter of the alphabet.
10. In Welsh, "llanfairpwllgwyngyllgogerychwyrndrobwllllantysiliogogogoch" is a town's name that translates to "The church of St. Mary in a hollow of white hazel near a rapid whirlpool and the church of St. Tysilio near the red cave."
11. The word "OK" is one of the most widely understood and used words in the world.
12. The sentence "Buffalo buffalo Buffalo buffalo buffalo buffalo Buffalo buffalo" is grammatically correct and means "Bison from Buffalo, New York, who are intimidated by other bison, intimidate other bison from Buffalo, New York."
13. The word "queue" is the only English word that is still pronounced the same way when the last four letters are removed.
14. The Hawaiian alphabet only has 13 letters.
15. The word "pangram" refers to a sentence that contains every letter of the alphabet at least once.
16. There are more English words beginning with the letter "s" than any other letter.
17. The sentence "I am" is the shortest complete sentence in the English language.
18. The sentence "Go!" is the shortest grammatically correct sentence in English.

19. The word "uncopyrightable" is the longest English word without repeating any letters.

20. The word "serendipity" was coined by Horace Walpole in 1754.

21. The word "alphabetical" is the longest word in the English language with all its letters in alphabetical order.

22. The word "book" is one of the most commonly used nouns in the English language.

23. The word "dreamt" is the only English word that ends in "mt."

24. The word "set" has the highest number of different meanings in the English language.

25. The sentence "A man, a plan, a canal, Panama!" is a palindrome, meaning it reads the same backward as forward.

26. The word "computer" was originally a job title for people who performed calculations.

27. The word "oxymoron" is itself an oxymoron, as it is derived from two Greek words meaning "sharp" and "dull."

28. The word "palindrome" is derived from the Greek words "palin," meaning "again," and "dromos," meaning "way" or "direction."

29. The longest word in the English language, according to the Oxford English Dictionary, is "pneumonoultramicroscopicsilicovolcanoconiosis," a lung disease caused by inhaling very fine silica particles.

30. The word "goodbye" is a contraction of the phrase "God be with you."

31. The word "alphabet" is a combination of the first two letters of the Greek alphabet: alpha and beta.

32. The sentence "The quick brown fox jumps over a lazy dog" is a pangram, meaning it uses every letter of the alphabet.

33. The word "language" is derived from the Latin word "lingua," which means "tongue."

34. The sentence "The rat the cat the dog chased killed ate the malt" is an example of a garden path sentence, where the reader is initially led down the wrong syntactic path.

35. The word "girl" was originally gender-neutral and meant a young person of either sex.

36. The word "syzygy" has three Ys and means the alignment of three celestial objects.

37. The sentence "James, while John had had 'had,' had had 'had had'; 'had had' had had the teacher's approval" is grammatically correct.

38. The sentence "Colorless green ideas sleep furiously" is grammatically correct but semantically nonsensical, coined by Noam Chomsky to demonstrate the difference between syntax and semantics.

39. The word "verb" is a noun.

40. The sentence "Buffalo buffalo Buffalo buffalo buffalo buffalo Buffalo buffalo" is grammatically correct and means "Buffalo bison that Buffalo bison intimidate, intimidate Buffalo bison."

41. The word "lisp" is ironic because people who have a lisp struggle to pronounce it.

42. The word "almost" is the longest word in the English language with all the letters in alphabetical order.

43. The word "uncopyrightable" is the longest English word with no repeated letters.

44. The word "uncopyrightable" is the longest English word with no repeating letters.

45. The word "ambidextrous" comes from the Latin words "ambidexter," meaning "right-handed on both sides," and "ambidextra," meaning "double-dealer."

46. The word "nerd" was first coined by Dr. Seuss in "If I Ran the Zoo."

47. The word "isogram" refers to a word or phrase in which no letter occurs more than once.

48. The word "alphabet" comes from the first two letters of the Greek alphabet, "alpha" and "beta."

49. The sentence "The quick brown fox jumps over a lazy dog" is known as a pangram.

50. The sentence "Able was I ere I saw Elba" is a famous palindrome attributed to Napoleon.

51. The word "bookkeeper" (and its variants) is the only unhyphenated English word with three consecutive double letters.

52. The sentence "The six slippery snails slid slowly seaward" is an example of alliteration.

53. The word "language" is derived from the Latin word "lingua," meaning "tongue."

54. The word "lollipop" is a blend of "lolly," a dialect word for the tongue, and "pop," which means slap.

55. The sentence "The rain in Spain stays mainly in the plain" is a famous line from the musical "My Fair Lady."

56. The sentence "James, while John had had 'had,' had had 'had had'; 'had had' had had the teacher's approval" is grammatically correct.

57. The word "dreamt" is the only English word that ends in "mt."

58. The word "onomatopoeia" is itself an example of onomatopoeia, as it imitates the sound it describes.

59. The word "pangram" refers to a sentence that contains every letter of the alphabet.

60. The sentence "A man, a plan, a canal, Panama!" is a palindrome.

61. The word "onomatopoeia" refers to words that imitate the sounds they describe.

62. The sentence "The rat the cat the dog chased killed ate the malt" is an example of a garden path sentence.

63. The word "lisp" is ironic because people with a lisp struggle to pronounce it.

64. The word "set" has the highest number of different meanings in the English language.

65. The word "uncopyrightable" is the longest English word without repeating any letters.

66. The word "serendipity" was coined by Horace Walpole in 1754.

67. The word "palindrome" is derived from the Greek words "palin," meaning "again," and "dromos," meaning "way" or "direction."

68. The longest word in the English language, according to the Oxford English Dictionary, is "pneumonoultramicroscopicsilicovolcanoconiosis," a lung disease caused by inhaling very fine silica particles.

69. The word "goodbye" is a contraction of the phrase "God be with you."

70. The word "syzygy" has three Ys and means the alignment of three celestial objects.

8

Movie

1. The first movie ever made is "Roundhay Garden Scene," filmed in Leeds, England, in 1888.
2. The word "nerd" was coined by Dr. Seuss in "If I Ran the Zoo."
3. The highest-grossing film of all time (as of my knowledge cutoff in 2022) is "Avatar."
4. The longest-running TV show is "The Simpsons," which has been on the air since 1989.
5. The first feature-length animated film is Disney's "Snow White and the Seven Dwarfs."
6. "Casablanca" holds the record for the most reissued movie.
7. The iconic Wilhelm Scream has been used in over 400 films.
8. Marilyn Monroe's real name was Norma Jeane Mortenson.
9. The first music video aired on MTV was "Video Killed the Radio Star" by The Buggles.
10. The word "smurf" is used as a noun, verb, and adjective in the Smurf language.
11. Stanley Kubrick's "The Shining" holds the record for the most retakes of a single scene.
12. The longest-running Broadway show is "The Phantom of the Opera."
13. The average person blinks about 15–20 times per minute—less during a movie.
14. "Psycho" was the first American film to feature a toilet flushing.
15. Alfred Hitchcock never won an Academy Award for Best Director.
16. "Titanic" spent more than two years in theaters worldwide.
17. The term "Blockbuster" originally referred to bombs during World War II.
18. The original name of the band U2 was "Feedback."
19. The first movie with a 3D version was "Bwana Devil" in 1952.
20. James Cameron wrote "Terminator" while living in his car.
21. Harrison Ford wasn't George Lucas's first choice for Han Solo.
22. The shortest war in history lasted 38–45 minutes between Britain and Zanzibar.
23. The first music video ever played on MTV Europe was "Money for Nothing" by Dire Straits.

24. Charlie Chaplin once entered a Charlie Chaplin look-alike contest and came in third.

25. The movie "Forrest Gump" was based on a novel of the same name.

26. The "Waffle House Index" is used by FEMA to assess hurricane damage.

27. "Pulp Fiction" was originally written to be a trio of stories released as a book.

28. The first recorded instance of special effects in movies dates back to 1857.

29. The first recorded instance of product placement in movies was for Ovaltine in 1934's "The Little Colonel."

30. The first film to show a flushing toilet was Alfred Hitchcock's "Psycho."

31. The longest running animated TV show is "Sazae-san," a Japanese series that premiered in 1969.

32. The famous MGM lion's roar at the beginning of movies is not a real lion but a sound effect.

33. The world's largest film studio is in Ramoji Film City, Hyderabad, India.

34. Tom Hanks provided the voice for Woody in "Toy Story" because his son loved the character.

35. The first film ever made in Hollywood was "In Old California" in 1910.

36. The shortest performance ever to win an Oscar was Anthony Hopkins in "The Silence of the Lambs" at 24 minutes.

37. The "D" in D-Day stands for "Day," making it "Day-Day."

38. The first video uploaded to YouTube was titled "Me at the zoo" by Jawed Karim.

39. The first film to use the term "OMG" was "1917."

40. The record for the most Oscar wins goes to Walt Disney with 22 awards.

41. The first color feature film was "Becky Sharp" in 1935.

42. The world's largest collection of movie memorabilia is in the Museo Nazionale del Cinema in Turin, Italy.

43. The longest-running sitcom is "The Adventures of Ozzie and Harriet."

44. The "X" in "X-ray" stands for "unknown."

45. "The Twilight Zone" was the first TV show to feature a flushing toilet.

46. The first film to gross over $1 billion worldwide was "Titanic."

47. The first movie with a soundtrack was "Don Juan" in 1926.

48. The most expensive film ever made is "Pirates of the Caribbean: On Stranger Tides."

49. The first movie to use the word "vampire" was "Nosferatu" in 1922.

50. The highest-grossing film directed by a woman is "Frozen," directed by Jennifer Lee and Chris Buck.

51. The first movie to be adapted from a video game was "Super Mario Bros." in 1993.

52. The longest film ever made is "Logistics," with a runtime of 51 days.

53. The first movie with a 3D sex scene is "The Stewardesses" in 1969.

54. The longest-running TV talk show is "The Tonight Show Starring Johnny Carson."

55. The first film to show a computer-generated image was "Westworld" in 1973.

56. The "Indiana Jones" character was named after George Lucas's dog.

57. The first movie to show a human kiss was "The Kiss" in 1896.

58. The first actor to portray James Bond was Barry Nelson in a 1954 TV adaptation of "Casino Royale."

59. The world's oldest surviving film is "Roundhay Garden Scene" from 1888.

60. The first film to win all five major Academy Awards was "It Happened One Night" in 1934.

61. The longest film without a script is "Russian Ark," shot in one continuous take.

62. The first movie with a recorded soundtrack was "The Jazz Singer" in 1927.

63. The first film to show a car chase was "The French Connection" in 1971.

64. The longest-running film festival is the Venice Film Festival, established in 1932.

65. The first movie to use the word "hello" was Thomas Edison's "The Hello Operator" in 1888.

66. The first movie to show a flushing toilet in the United States was "The Great Train Robbery" in 1903.

67. The first film with a post-credits scene was "Master of the World" in 1961.

68. The most expensive movie ticket ever sold was for "Titanic 3D" at $2,500.

69. The first film to win the "Big Five" Oscars was "It Happened One Night" in 1934.

70. The first film to use Technicolor was "Becky Sharp" in 1935.

9

Pop

1. Michael Jackson's album "Thriller" is the best-selling album of all time, with over 66 million copies sold worldwide.
2. The first music video ever played on MTV was "Video Killed the Radio Star" by The Buggles.
3. Elvis Presley, often referred to as the "King of Rock and Roll," didn't write any of his songs.
4. The longest-running No. 1 song on the Billboard Hot 100 is "One Sweet Day" by Mariah Carey and Boyz II Men, holding the spot for 16 weeks.
5. The Beatles hold the record for the most No. 1 hits on the Billboard Hot 100.
6. The term "rock and roll" was originally a slang term for sex in African American communities.
7. Bob Marley's song "One Love" was designated the Song of the Millennium by the BBC in 1999.
8. Beyoncé is the most nominated woman in the history of the Grammy Awards.
9. The word "pop" in pop music stands for "popular."
10. Lady Gaga got her stage name from the Queen song "Radio Ga Ga."
11. The piano used in the song "Imagine" by John Lennon was later sold for over $2 million.
12. Freddie Mercury, the lead singer of Queen, had a degree in art and graphic design.
13. The synthesizer was first introduced in pop music by The Beach Boys in the 1960s.
14. The first music video to air on MTV featuring an African American artist was Michael Jackson's "Billie Jean."
15. Adele's "21" is the best-selling album of the 21st century in the UK.
16. Madonna's birth name is Madonna Louise Ciccone.
17. The song "Happy Birthday to You" is one of the highest-earning songs of all time.
18. The first Grammy Awards were held in 1959.
19. Jimi Hendrix played his guitar upside down because he was left-handed.

20. The guitar riff in Nirvana's "Smells Like Teen Spirit" was meant to mimic Boston's "More Than a Feeling."
21. The Spice Girls' debut single "Wannabe" became the best-selling single by a girl group of all time.
22. Prince could play 27 instruments.
23. The Rolling Stones' "Satisfaction" was their first No. 1 hit in the United States.
24. The Bee Gees wrote and produced all of the songs on the "Saturday Night Fever" soundtrack.
25. The first music streaming service was created in 1897 when people could dial in to listen to music over the phone.
26. The first music video played on MTV Europe was "Money for Nothing" by Dire Straits.
27. Rihanna's "Umbrella" was originally written for Britney Spears.
28. The "M" in MTV originally stood for "Music," but as the channel diversified its programming, it was officially changed to MTV.
29. The concept of autotune was first used by Cher in her 1998 song "Believe."
30. The most expensive music video ever made is Michael and Janet Jackson's "Scream," costing $7 million.
31. The electric guitar was invented in 1931.
32. Whitney Houston's version of "I Will Always Love You" is one of the best-selling singles of all time.
33. The first music video to reach 1 billion views on YouTube was "Gangnam Style" by PSY.
34. ABBA's "Dancing Queen" was the first song to have a music video.
35. The longest song ever recorded is "In-a-Gadda-da-Vida" by Iron Butterfly, with a runtime of over 17 minutes.
36. The Beatles used the word "love" 613 times in their songs.
37. The world's largest record collection is owned by Paul Mawhinney, with over three million records.
38. Elvis Presley's "Heartbreak Hotel" was his first No. 1 hit.
39. The first commercially successful compact disc was Billy Joel's "52nd Street."
40. The synthesizer riff in Europe's "Final Countdown" was originally meant to be a soundcheck warm-up.
41. Madonna has sold over 300 million records worldwide.
42. The longest concert by a solo artist lasted over 32 hours and was performed by Prasanna Gudi.
43. The longest-running musical on Broadway is "The Phantom of the Opera."

44. The first music video played on MTV Asia was "Too Legit to Quit" by MC Hammer.
45. The song "Hey Jude" by The Beatles was originally titled "Hey Jules" and was written for John Lennon's son, Julian.
46. The first music video filmed in space was David Bowie's "Space Oddity" by Canadian astronaut Chris Hadfield.
47. "Bohemian Rhapsody" by Queen is the only song to have been No. 1 twice with the same version.
48. The first rap song to win a Grammy was "Parents Just Don't Understand" by DJ Jazzy Jeff & The Fresh Prince.
49. The word "rap" is an acronym for "rhythm and poetry."
50. The first CD ever pressed was "The Visitors" by ABBA.
51. The Beatles' rooftop concert in London was their last public performance.
52. Elvis Presley made over 30 movies during his career.
53. The first music video ever made was for Queen's "Bohemian Rhapsody."
54. The world's largest music festival is Summerfest in Milwaukee, USA.
55. Led Zeppelin's "Stairway to Heaven" is often considered one of the greatest rock songs ever.
56. The first music video played on MTV Latin America was "Money" by Pink Floyd.
57. The piano used by John Lennon to write "Imagine" was later bought by George Michael.
58. ABBA's song "Fernando" was the group's only No. 1 hit in the United States.
59. The first music video played on MTV Africa was "Pump It" by The Black Eyed Peas.
60. The longest-running No. 1 song in the United States is "Old Town Road" by Lil Nas X, holding the spot for 19 weeks.
61. The word "jazz" was originally a slang term for sexual intercourse.
62. The first music video played on MTV India was "Whatcha Say" by Jason Derulo.
63. The first music video played on MTV Japan was "Dare" by Gorillaz.
64. Madonna's "Like a Virgin" was her first No. 1 hit on the Billboard Hot 100.
65. The first music video played on MTV Australia was "Straight Lines" by Silverchair.
66. The song "Lose Yourself" by Eminem is the first rap song to win an Academy Award for Best Original Song.
67. The first music video played on MTV China was "Let It Rock" by Kevin Rudolf.

68. The first music video played on MTV Russia was "I'm with Stupid" by Pet Shop Boys.

69. The longest-running No. 1 song on the UK Singles Chart is "Someone You Loved" by Lewis Capaldi, holding the spot for seven weeks.

70. The first music video played on MTV Korea was "Hot Issue" by 4Minute.

10

Science

1. The speed of light is approximately 299,792 kilometers per second.

2. Honey never spoils; archaeologists have found pots of honey in ancient Egyptian tombs that are over 3,000 years old and still perfectly edible.

3. The Earth's core is hotter than the surface of the sun.

4. A teaspoonful of neutron star material would weigh about 6 billion tons on Earth.

5. Octopuses have three hearts: two pump blood to the gills, and one pumps it to the rest of the body.

6. The average human body carries about 4 pounds of bacteria.

7. The universe is 13.8 billion years old.

8. A day on Venus is longer than a year on Venus. It rotates on its axis once every 243 Earth days but takes about 225 Earth days to orbit the sun.

9. There are more possible iterations of a game of chess than there are atoms in the observable universe.

10. The human brain is capable of generating about 20 watts of electrical power.

11. Sound can't travel through a vacuum, which is why there is no sound in space.

12. If you could fold a piece of paper 42 times, it would reach the moon.

13. The largest known star, UY Scuti, is over 1,700 times the size of the sun.

14. A single rainforest can produce 20% of the Earth's oxygen.

15. The Great Wall of China is not visible from the moon with the naked eye.

16. A lightning bolt is hotter than the surface of the sun.

17. The human body has more than 600 muscles.

18. The word "nerd" was first coined by Dr. Seuss in "If I Ran the Zoo."

19. The Eiffel Tower can be 15 cm taller during the summer due to thermal expansion.

20. The shortest war in history was between Britain and Zanzibar on August 27, 1896, lasting only 38 minutes.

21. Wombat poop is cube-shaped.

22. Cows have best friends.

23. A group of flamingos is called a "flamboyance."

24. The smell of freshly-cut grass is actually a plant distress call.

25. The electric chair was invented by a dentist.

26. Honeybees can recognize human faces.

27. Cows have regional accents.

28. Bananas are berries, but strawberries aren't.

29. A single raindrop can fall at speeds of up to 22 miles per hour.

30. The longest time between two twins being born is 87 days.

31. A day on Mars is only about 24.6 hours.

32. The longest word without a vowel is "rhythms."

33. Only female mosquitoes bite.

34. There are more possible iterations of a game of chess than there are atoms in the observable universe.

35. The shortest war in history was between Britain and Zanzibar on August 27, 1896, lasting only 38 minutes.

36. The world's largest desert is Antarctica.

37. The human eye is capable of distinguishing about 10 million different colors.

38. A "jiffy" is an actual unit of time: 1/100th of a second.

39. The longest word in the English language without a vowel is "rhythms."

40. Jupiter's mass is two and a half times that of all the other planets in the solar system combined.

41. The first computer mouse was made of wood.

42. A single strand of spaghetti is called a "spaghetto."

43. A piece of paper cannot be folded more than 13 times.

44. The word "astronaut" comes from the Greek words "astron," meaning star, and "nautes," meaning sailor.

45. The Great Wall of China is not visible from the moon with the naked eye.

46. Humans and giraffes have the same number of neck vertebrae.

47. The "D" in D-Day stands for "Day." The term is used in military planning to denote the day on which a combat attack or operation is set to commence.

48. A "butt" was a medieval unit of measure for wine.

49. The first 3D movie was released in 1922.

50. The word "bookkeeper" (and its variants) is the only unhyphenated English word with three consecutive double letters.

51. The shortest war in history was between Britain and Zanzibar on August 27, 1896, lasting only 38 minutes.

52. The longest time between two twins being born is 87 days.

53. The world's largest desert is Antarctica.

54. The first recorded game of baseball was played in 1846 in Hoboken, New Jersey.

55. There are more possible iterations of a game of chess than there are atoms in the observable universe.

56. Octopuses have three hearts: two pump blood to the gills, and one pumps it to the rest of the body.

57. The longest word without a vowel is "rhythms."

58. A day on Venus is longer than a year on Venus. It rotates on its axis once every 243 Earth days but takes about 225 Earth days to orbit the sun.

59. A "jiffy" is an actual unit of time: 1/100th of a second.

60. The Earth's core is hotter than the surface of the sun.

61. Honey never spoils; archaeologists have found pots of honey in ancient Egyptian tombs that are over 3,000 years old and still perfectly edible.

62. The first computer mouse was made of wood.

63. A piece of paper cannot be folded more than 13 times.

64. The word "bookkeeper" (and its variants) is the only unhyphenated English word with three consecutive double letters.

65. The first recorded game of baseball was played in 1846 in Hoboken, New Jersey.

66. The Great Wall of China is not visible from the moon with the naked eye.

67. A "butt" was a medieval unit of measure for wine.

68. The electric chair was invented by a dentist.

69. Humans and giraffes have the same number of neck vertebrae.

70. The "D" in D-Day stands for "Day." The term is used in military planning to denote the day on which a combat attack or operation is set to commence.

11

Strangest creatures

1. The axolotl, a salamander, can regrow entire limbs and even parts of its heart and brain.
2. The immortal jellyfish can revert its cells to their earliest form and start its life cycle anew.
3. The mimic octopus can imitate the appearance and behaviors of various sea creatures to avoid predators.
4. The fang tooth fish has the largest teeth in proportion to its body size of any fish.
5. The mantis shrimp has the fastest punch in the animal kingdom, reaching speeds of 50 mph.
6. The blob fish looks strange out of water, but in its deep-sea habitat, it appears more normal due to pressure.
7. The aye-aye, a lemur from Madagascar, has a long, thin middle finger used for tapping on trees to find insects.
8. The blue dragon sea slug is a small but vibrant creature with a beautiful and deadly sting.
9. The narwhal, often called the "unicorn of the sea," has a long, spiral tusk that can reach lengths of 10 feet.
10. The platypus is one of the few mammals that lay eggs instead of giving birth to live young.
11. The mimicry of leaf-tailed geckos allows them to blend seamlessly with their surroundings.
12. The immortal hydra, a tiny freshwater creature, can regenerate its entire body from just a small piece.
13. The pink fairy armadillo is the smallest armadillo species and has a pinkish shell.
14. The frilled-neck lizard opens its mouth wide and displays a frill around its neck as a defense mechanism.
15. The fang fish has sharp, needle-like teeth and a light-producing lure to attract prey in the deep sea.
16. The shoe bill bird has a massive shoe-shaped bill and is known for its intimidating appearance.

17. The tarsier has eyes larger than its brain and can rotate its head 180 degrees.
18. The star-nosed mole has a bizarre star-shaped appendage on its nose, used for sensing prey.
19. The blue-ringed octopus carries enough venom to kill 26 humans within minutes.
20. The proboscis monkey has a long, droopy nose that can grow up to 7 inches.
21. The Venezuelan poodle moth has a fluffy appearance and is still a mystery to scientists.
22. The hammer-headed bat has an unusually large head with a hammer-shaped structure.
23. The axolotl is a neotenic salamander, meaning it retains its aquatic larval features throughout adulthood.
24. The ghost pipefish resembles floating seaweed and is a master of camouflage.
25. The dumbo octopus has ear-like fins, giving it a resemblance to the Disney character Dumbo.
26. The barreleye fish has a transparent head, allowing it to see through the top of its skull.
27. The star-nosed mole can detect and consume prey in as little as 227 milliseconds.
28. The goblin shark can extend its jaw to capture prey with incredible speed.
29. The red-lipped batfish walks on the ocean floor using its pectoral fins.
30. The mata mata turtle has a unique appearance with a flat, triangular head and a long neck.
31. The leaf sheep sea slug looks like a grazing sheep and can photosynthesize using stolen chloroplasts.
32. The gliding snake can flatten its body to glide between trees, similar to flying squirrels.
33. The jerboa has long hind legs and a kangaroo-like jump, making it an excellent jumper.
34. The aye-aye has an elongated middle finger used for extracting insects from tree bark.
35. The umbrella bird has a black crest on its head that opens like an umbrella during courtship displays.
36. The blobfish's gelatinous appearance is due to its lack of a swim bladder, allowing it to live at extreme depths.
37. The leaf-tailed gecko can change colors and patterns to match its surroundings.
38. The Japanese spider crab has the longest leg span of any arthropod, reaching up to 12 feet.

39. The thorny devil lizard has a false head on the back of its neck to confuse predators.

40. The blue glaucus sea slug can absorb and concentrate the venom of its prey for self-defense.

41. The lamprey is a jawless fish that attaches itself to other fish and feeds on their blood.

42. The hagfish produces slime as a defense mechanism, clogging the gills of potential predators.

43. The tube-nosed fruit bat has a tube-like structure on its nose, resembling a straw.

44. The sarcastic fringehead has an exaggerated mouth that it uses for territorial disputes.

45. The peacock mantis shrimp has complex eyes and can see polarized light.

46. The thorny dragon lizard can collect water through its skin and direct it towards its mouth.

47. The tucuxi, a type of river dolphin, can navigate through flooded forests during the wet season.

48. The star-nosed mole's unique nose has 22 fleshy appendages, each equipped with touch receptors.

49. The blue-ringed octopus displays its vibrant colors as a warning when threatened.

50. The giraffe-necked weevil has an elongated neck, which males use for combat over mates.

51. The gulper eel has a large, hinged mouth that allows it to swallow prey much larger than itself.

52. The yeti crab is covered in hair-like structures and thrives near hydrothermal vents on the ocean floor.

53. The barreleye fish has upward-facing eyes that can rotate to see prey above.

54. The thorny dragon lizard has spines covering its body, providing protection from predators.

55. The fang tooth fish has teeth so large that it can't close its mouth fully.

56. The gulper eel has a bioluminescent lure at the end of its tail to attract prey in the dark depths.

57. The flying snake flattens its body to glide between trees, using its ribs to create an aerodynamic shape.

58. The axolotl is often used in scientific research for its regenerative abilities.

59. The coconut crab, the largest terrestrial arthropod, can climb trees and crack open coconuts with its powerful claws.

60. The mantis shrimp's punch is so powerful that it can break the glass of an aquarium.

61. The thorny devil lizard uses capillary action to draw water from the ground into its mouth.

62. The tube-nosed fruit bat plays a crucial role in pollinating flowers in its native habitat.

63. The leaf sheep sea slug's resemblance to a sheep is enhanced by its frilly appendages.

64. The axolotl is critically endangered in the wild due to habitat loss and pollution.

65. The mimic octopus can imitate the appearance and movements of lionfish, flatfish, and sea snakes.

66. The fang fish has a bioluminescent lure that dangles in front of its mouth to attract prey.

67. The barreleye fish's transparent head protects its sensitive eyes from the sharp spines of its prey.

68. The narwhal's tusk is actually a long, spiral tooth that can reach lengths of up to 10 feet.

www.ingramcontent.com/pod-product-compliance
Lightning Source LLC
Chambersburg PA
CBHW060855260726
48661CB00008B/3270